THE BURE VALLEY RAILWAY

ANDY STANSFIELD

HALSGROVE

First published in Great Britain in 2008

Copyright © Andy Stansfield 2008

Title page: No.7 Spitfire about to be passed by No.1 Wroxham Broad at Brampton loop.

British Library Cataloguing-in-Publication Data
A CIP record for this title is available from the British Library

ISBN 978 1 84114 800 7

HALSGROVE
Halsgrove House,
Ryelands Industrial Estate,
Bagley Road, Wellington, Somerset TA21 9PZ
Tel: 01823 653777   Fax: 01823 216796
email: sales@halsgrove.com
website: www.halsgrove.com

Printed and bound by Grafiche Flaminia, Italy

No.6 Blickling Hall at Coltishall Station.

INTRODUCTION

The setting for this delightful narrow gauge railway is undoubtedly one of its great attractions and it is no surprise that it is marketed as The Bure Valley Railway Experience. Not only can visitors enjoy an invigorating ride on a steam train, they can link up with a variety of attractions in the area such as a boat trip on the Norfolk Broads, a visit to the historic Blickling Hall, a browse around Hoveton Hall Gardens or just a gentle walk and a picnic beside the River Bure.

Built in 1990, the line itself runs for nine miles between Aylsham, where the operation is based, and Wroxham. It follows the former trackbed of the East Norfolk Railway dating back to 1880. In between the two small towns are three stations at Brampton, Buxton and Coltishall. The first two are just halts with a short platform, whereas Coltishall has a considerably longer platform because the station also serves as one of three loops which allow trains travelling in opposite directions to pass one another on what is otherwise a single-track line.

The vast majority of travellers along the line board at Aylsham and choose a return trip all the way to Wroxham, a journey of three-quarters of an hour in each direction. This is a rewarding experience and Wroxham is a pleasant place to wander around and enjoy a relaxed lunch, even if you don't take up the option of a boat trip on the Broads. Even the countless cyclists and walkers, making use of the path which accompanies the track along its entire length, tend to complete the full nine miles then travel back by train. But this leaves a great many other options unexplored along the central portion of the line. The riverside inn at Coltishall, for example, is situated in one of the finest locations imaginable for lunch. The footpath along the banks of the Bure from Brampton to Buxton, passing the riverside church at Lamas and picturesque Oxnead, is also a wonderful excuse for making use of these intermediate stations.

Although the Bure Valley Railway operates during twelve months of the year, services are obviously restricted during the winter months but there are still special events to watch out for, such as Santa Specials. At other times of the year there are half-price offers for Mother's Day and Father's Day, gala weekends and Days Out With Thomas. It is also possible to join one of the Driver Experience Courses so that you can learn first-hand what it is like to pilot one of these narrow gauge engineering marvels.

But keeping these locomotives and their rolling stock functioning requires constant attention and a dedicated team of full-time staff and volunteers, many of whom are capable of turning their hand to many different tasks. The team ethic is incredibly strong and on the following pages you will see the General Manager pushing a loco around on the turntable, drivers acting as guards, and engineers ferrying buckets of coal. In particular, the small group of full-time staff are as flexible as they are enthusiastic but they couldn't run the railway without the large number of trained volunteers. They all have one thing in common, however, and that is their obvious sense of pleasure in their job, something which they pass on to the travelling public in liberal doses.

Drivers will regale interested visitors with some of the more unusual sights along the line, too. Between them they have seen foxes, roe and muntjack deer, occasional marsh harriers and kingfishers, stoats and weasels, and around a dozen pairs of green woodpeckers along the line. They have seen countless slow worms when cutting grass on the embankments and found lizards sleeping beneath the sleepers, not to mention spotting tawny, barn and little owls, occasionally perched on fence posts beside the track.

By now the reader will have begun to understand why this line is heralded as The Bure Valley Experience and is so much more than merely a steam enthusiast's great day out. The images on the pages which follow are intended to add to that appreciation of the experience and, hopefully, entice the reader to keep coming back.

Andy Stansfield

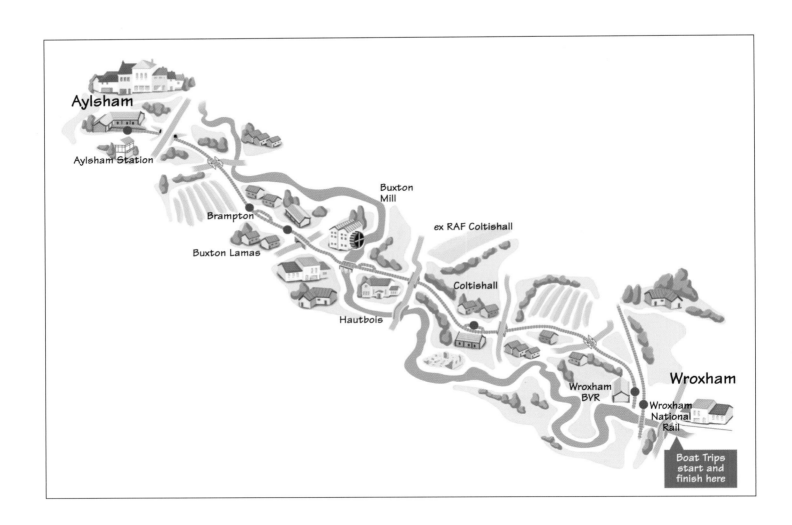

Aylsham

Aylsham Station

Brampton

Buxton Lamas

Buxton Mill

ex RAF Coltishall

Coltishall

Hautbois

Wroxham

Wroxham BVR

Wroxham National Rail

Boat Trips start and finish here

Coltishall loop

No.9 Mark Timothy leaving Coltishall loop on the way to Wroxham. This is one of three places on this single-track line where 'up' and 'down' trains can pass one another.

Summer afternoon
No.7 Spitfire with the 13.17 departure southbound from Coltishall. Trains during the middle
of the day tend to be much less busy than their morning and teatime counterparts.

Brampton loop

The bright blue colour scheme of No.1 Wroxham Broad makes it easily identifiable as it passes through Brampton loop heading for Wroxham while the northbound train waits patiently at a standstill.

All aboard

Aylsham passengers make the most of the ten minutes before departure with a good look at their loco while waiting to take the first steam service of the day to Wroxham. The first and last service each day is always pulled by a diesel.

Old Post House, Brampton
This attractive cottage can be found at the corner of the road to Aylsham and
the winding lane which leads to Upper Brampton with its attractive church.

Wroxham turntable
Full-time staff need to be prepared to carry out a wide variety of tasks: here the General Manager is acting as driver on the first service of the day which means that he also gets to operate the manual turntable too.

Opposite:
Aylsham turntable
There are turntables at both ends of the line, each within view of the platforms. The railway's only female full-time driver, Juliet Walker, pushes the 13 ton Blickling Hall round with ease.

Marsham
The small village of Marsham lies a couple of miles due south of Aylsham.

Northbound
No.1 Wroxham Broad heading for Aylsham on a sunny summer's day which
makes its Caledonian Sky Blue colour scheme look even more vibrant.

Screen break

A vital member of the office staff, Judith Harvey, takes a breather on Aylsham's colourful platform. Both tubs and hanging baskets decorate the platforms, their regular watering being one more job on an already varied list for the few full-time staff.

Opposite:
Floral tribute

No.8 Thunder makes its first formal appearance for three years, though with less drama than its name suggests, following lengthy repairs and alterations.

A clear message
The few level crossings on the line are all on minor roads but safety is still essential.
This crossing is at Spratt's Green just a few minutes' train journey south of Aylsham.

Belaugh Green

Situated just north of Wroxham, the level crossing at Belaugh (pronounced 'be-low') Green is ungated, as indeed are all the crossings on the line. Blickling Hall creeps over the crossing which is immediately adjacent to a T-junction which makes it even more essential for the driver to be aware of the traffic.

Buxton to Oxnead

On the north side of Buxton Station a footpath signposted to Oxnead Church carries walkers across these fields to the picturesque village of Oxnead from which a riverside footpath can be taken to Brampton.

Opposite:

Crimson blur

The final leg between Brampton and Aylsham is one of the fastest stretches of track. As it passes fields awaiting harvest, No.6 Blickling Hall briefly appears as a crimson blur where it peeks out above the crops and the field boundary. There is a maximum speed limit of 20mph along the entire line.

Unmistakeable
The distinctive spotlight adorning the front of No.9 Mark Timothy makes it easy to identify.
Observant readers may have spotted Mark Timothy badged as No.10 during the
years 1999 (when it was built) and 2005 when it was re-numbered.

Two wheeled fun

The path which runs adjacent to the line throughout its entire length is deservedly popular with cyclists of all ages and levels of fitness. As the path is shared with pedestrians, it is a good idea to have a bell fitted to your bike.

Relative speed
A lone cyclist overtakes No.1 Wroxham Broad as it slowly gathers momentum on leaving Wroxham Station.
The train will take 45 minutes to reach Aylsham, the average cyclist perhaps an hour.

Wroxham
The view from Wroxham's renowned bridge. The brightly coloured
boats on the right are 'day boats' which can be hired by the hour.

Top up
Buckets are filled with coal and lined up
ready for refuelling the steam locos when
they turn around at Aylsham.

Pit stop
No.8 Thunder is refuelled before setting off for Wroxham. Passengers get a close view of many minor tasks which are carried out on the locos during the course of the day.

Yard pilot

No.4 is a three ton 0-4-0 loco whose main job is described as being a 'yard pilot'. It has a Peugeot diesel engine and is used in conjunction with the specially built flail to maintain the trackside, when protective mesh is added to its windows for safety.

Flail
This specially constructed device, pulled by No.4, has greatly aided the management of the trackside and can be used for spraying as well as grass cutting. It came into service in April 2003.
Photo courtesy of Neal Cumming.

The Harrods connection

This lathe, made by Dean Smith & Grace in Keighley in 1955, was purchased by Eastern Region for £1255/12/6d. The BVR acquired it ten years ago from a company in nearby Swaffham where it had been used for turning hat stands for Harrods. Today it is used for a variety of jobs but especially wheel turning.

No.8 Thunder detail

Mid-morning encounter
No.7 Spitfire meets up with the diesel No.3 as it returns from Wroxham on the first service of the day.

Coltishall

Next to the River Bure at Coltishall there is a huge expanse of grass which is a favoured picnic spot or you could treat yourself to lunch at the riverside pub.

Approaching Little Hautbois
No.6 Blickling Hall passing one of the copses on the north
side of the line on this stretch approaching Little Hautbois
(pronounced 'hobbis').

Opposite:
River Bure and swans
Where the line crosses the Bure on the edge of Buxton there are
steps leading down to the riverside footpath which can be
followed along this stretch down to Coltishall via Little Hautbois.

35

Elegance
Not as fast as the famous fighter aircraft but just as elegant, Spitfire leaves Buxton at 15.42 on its way to Wroxham.

Santa Special
A great favourite with both children and parents alike, Santa Specials run each year approaching Christmas. Here Santa swaps his reindeer for a ride on No. 7 Spitfire. *Photos left and opposite courtesy of Neal Cumming.*

38

Thomas Days

Thomas the Tank Engine Days are always fun. This shot shows No.1 Wroxham Broad acting out the role at New Romney. It is quite common for locos to be loaned out to other narrow gauge lines like Romney, Hythe & Dymchurch or the Ravenglass & Eskdale.

Volunteer guard
John Orton, one of many volunteers, takes on the important role of guard for the
day aboard the Ocean Mails guard's van No. 81, seen here at Wroxham.

Shade
Several sections of the line are well shaded by trees, especially where the track passes
through a cutting, which can be quite welcome on a hot summer day.

Spick and span
Volunteer driver Jeff Riley gives No.9 Mark Timothy a quick polish before departure.

Cliff Hilton

Another volunteer guard, Cliff is one of the many volunteers without whom the BVR would find it difficult to function. Volunteers are generally either guards or drivers but not both.

Entering Aylsham Station

Sighs of relief all round as No.8 Thunder arrives back at Aylsham successfully after its first
run pulling fare-paying passengers for three years following an extensive overhaul.

44

Wroxham turntable and signal box
The old signal box remains unused but the Wroxham Signalbox Trust plans
to turn the Grade II Listed Building into a small museum.

Platform 3 empty
Apart from two carriages the platforms are empty so it is easy to see the
extent to which potted plants and hanging baskets brighten up the station.

Opposite:
Platform 3
Families alight from No.8 Thunder at Aylsham. Beyond the
platform is some of the rolling stock awaiting refurbishment.

Departing Aylsham
On a lovely summer's day, with the flower bed by the signal box in the foreground,
Wroxham Broad carries passengers in exactly that direction.

Aylsham
This florist is one of many shops with character in this small market town.

Mark Timothy
No.9 sits patiently at Wroxham waiting to take the 12.45 service back to Aylsham.

Belaugh Green level crossing
Trains actually take the level crossings very slowly, but this slow exposure makes the point that it still takes only one second for the loco to traverse the width of the road.

Bure near Oxnead
The view eastwards along the River Bure from the bridge near Oxnead, a short walk from Brampton Station.

Riverside walk
There is a delightful walk along the river between Buxton and Brampton,
less than three miles in length from station to station.

Coach No. 9319

Constructed in 1989/90 with a colour scheme described as 'chocolate and cream' this lead carriage is pulled out of Aylsham by No.8 Thunder.

Crimson

Just over half the line's passenger coaches are either crimson or 'crimson lake' in colour.

Juliet

The name of the driver, not the loco. Juliet Walker is one of the full-time staff and revels in her job, seen her with the tank engine Wroxham Broad which doubles as Thomas the Tank Engine.

Opposite:
No. 8 detail

Just to keep spectators on their toes, the positioning of each loco's number varies. They are more easily identified by their colour.

Patience personified

Mark Timothy waits patiently at Coltishall loop, as does the driver, for the diesel No.3 which is a few minutes behind schedule. On a single-track line any delay affects trains in both directions. Normally timekeeping is excellent!

Held together by string

It's OK, this is not a reference to the locos or carriages, seen here at Brampton loop. If you look very closely you'll see a piece of string attached to the driver's cap and disappearing into his overalls. The other end is attached to his belt. Paul has lost so many caps that now he makes sure that they won't fly too far when blown off!

Above:
Ambition
Budding Station Masters can acquire at least
part of their uniform in the well-stocked shop.

Left:
Bear necessity
There are also lots of souvenirs for
younger visitors to take home.

Aylsham station shop
A huge selection of railway books is stocked, along with a wide range of model train accessories from three leading manufacturers, plus souvenirs for all ages.

Cornish visitors
This happy couple have travelled up from Plymouth to visit the line, to be rewarded with a week of glorious weather.

Steam 1
Passengers alight at Aylsham after travelling up on Steam 1's return leg from Wroxham.
The first and last services of the day are diesel hauled. The rest of the day is covered by
two steam locos turn and turn about, referred to as Steam 1 and Steam 2.

Oiling the wheels
A spot of routine maintenance before departure: Juliet Walker keeps the wheels turning on No.6 Blickling Hall.

Mind the doors!
Always on the lookout
for an unusual shot,
I arrived early for the
first service of the day
to find it waiting at
the platform with
every single carriage
door opened to the
same angle.

65

Approaching Wroxham
No.3 2nd Air Division USAAF about to enter Wroxham with the first service on yet another beautiful day.

Approaching Coltishall
Wroxham Broad heading north in the middle of the afternoon.

Boat Train
Spitfire hauls the Boat Train in the direction of Wroxham, seen here leaving
Coltishall loop with the northbound service disappearing into the distance.

Brampton loop
Mark Timothy swings back onto the single track at Brampton as Blickling Hall heads south pulling The Broadsman.

Pedigree
One of two fields containing these delightful Palomino ponies near Brampton, encountered when following the riverside path along the Bure near Oxnead.

Bure and ponies
The second tree-lined field of ponies, referred to above, can be seen in context next to the river. From this point there is also a much shorter route to Buxton Station instead of following the river, or to Oxnead Church in the opposite direction.

St Andrew's Church
The church at Lamas (also spelled Lammas) is situated on the banks of the River Bure and, unusually, the trees in the churchyard are mostly weeping willows.

Multi-tasking
Like many of the full-time staff of both sexes, Bob King is good at
taking on any of the wide range of duties which need to be attended to.

Spratt's Green
No.9 Mark Timothy departed from Aylsham just a few minutes before arriving at the Spratt's Green level crossing. The occupants of the house adjacent to the crossing have a fine view of the line from their front garden.

The Vintage Broadsman
Seen here entering Wroxham Broad, this is perhaps the most romantic of the craft used by
Broads Tours in conjunction with the line. A combined ticket can be purchased at the station.

No.7 Spitfire
The Boat Train carries passengers to Wroxham for the 11.30 sailing from Broads Tours'
base adjacent to the bridge in the centre of Wroxham, a 15 minute walk from the station.

Queen of the Broads
This craft provides good cover from the elements and is another used by
Broads Tours in conjunction with the Boat Train.

Disabled facilities

This lady in a wheelchair was kind enough to help out with this shot of the restaurant, which serves a wide range of drinks, snacks and hot meals during the day. The line has six special carriages which are fitted with double doors, ramps and low windows and are designed to facilitate wheelchair access and to seat a disabled person's carer. These coaches are available on every single train and are also useful for larger children's buggies and bicycles when not occupied by disabled persons.

Opposite:

All the action

The entrance to Aylsham Station sees quite a lot of activity. Clipboards are exchanged between the signal box and the driver or guard, the water tower on the left refills the locos, and just out of sight on the left lies the turntable.

Aylsham water tower

Martin Cogger tops up a loco with water at Aylsham. The water tower is deceiving in that it actually
contains a standard domestic header tank! It is mains fed through a water softener with added treatments
to help prevent corrosion. This loco's water capacity is a staggering 440 gallons and it maintains
a boiler pressure of 180 psi, roughly six times the pressure of your car tyres.

The Aylsham shuffle

When a train arrives at Aylsham it is detached from the carriages, reverses over a set of points onto a track parallel to the coaches and out of the station to just beyond the signal box. It then moves forwards onto the turntable and is manually rotated 180º before moving forwards again to beyond the points by the signal box. Finally it reverses back to the platform to attach the carriages once more, which is what No.6 Blickling Hall is doing here.

Wroxham Station and water tower
Unlike the platforms at Aylsham which are all covered by a roof, those at Wroxham are open which makes it much easier to obtain photos – but not so attractive if it's raining! Shortly after the photo shoot was finished there was a brief panic when the mains water supply to the water tower was interrupted. Now the full-time staff can add the role of plumber to the long list of driver, guard, radio operator, engineer . . .

Letting off steam

Despite occasional frustrations, the staff are a mild-mannered bunch and it is only the locos
which need to let off steam occasionally, like Mark Timothy just outside Wroxham Station.

Lamas
The tiny village of Lamas is situated just east of
Buxton and only a short walk from the station.

Opposite:
Parallel lives
While Mark Timothy and passengers enjoy the journey
northwards between Coltishall and Buxton, this family of swans
explore the Bure at a slower pace. The two run parallel to each
other for about three miles on this section of track.

Permission to proceed

Volunteer driver Jeff Riley on the radio to Control. No driver may move his or her train into any section of the line without being given specific permission to do so. Every instruction is repeated back from the receiver as a precaution and all transmissions are recorded.

Caution
Every carriage has warning notices about leaning out of the
window but enthusiasm sometimes gets the better of people.

The younger the better
A toddler is introduced to the joys of steam while Wroxham Broad is fed some
oil from its own personalised oil can, identified by a large yellow 1.

Gently does it
Juliet Walker cautiously backs up to the carriages waiting to ferry passengers
north again from the terminus at the southern end of the line.

Round the bend
The southbound entry into, and northbound exit from,
Coltishall Station is on a gradual bend which allows easier
photography of both the engine and the coaches behind it.

Opposite:
Mermaid bridge
Between Aylsham and Brampton the line crosses the Mermaid,
a watercourse which appears to be a man-made drainage
ditch. Despite asking numerous locals about the origin of
the name, no one came up with an explanation. Answers
on a postcard please . . .

Wroxham Barns
This Craft Centre is host to a wide range of shops and craftsmen and, despite the name,
is actually a couple of miles out of Wroxham itself not far from Hoveton Hall.

Parish Church of St Peter, Hoveton
Dating from 1624 this attractive little church is passed on the side road leading to Hoveton Hall Gardens.

Ballast
Most of us wouldn't give a second thought to what we might refer to as 'chippings' but there is
a science to laying ballast and it is gradually being upgraded as and when sections of the track are
worked on, along with replacement of the sleepers with hardwood ones of greater thickness.

Now when I say push . . .

. . . all I want you to do is shove 11 tons of steel, copper, brass, coal and water round so that it's facing the opposite way. Oh, and by the way, that doesn't include the weight of the turntable itself!

Ready for the off

The passengers are all on board, the doors are all closed, and the solitary figure of Bob King makes his way back to the guard's van. The traditional green flag is still used by the guard to let the driver know that he can depart.

Aylsham town centre
This scene is only a couple of minutes walk from the station. The signpost on
the left points the way to Blickling Hall, after which No.6 is named.

Mark Timothy at Coltishall
Of the five stations Coltishall is one of the easiest for taking photos of the trains.

The Broadsman
Spitfire waits at Brampton loop for permission via the radio to enter the next section of track.

Tank engine
The wideangle lens exaggerates perspective somewhat but the huge tanks on either side of the loco clearly indicate why this type of loco is designated a tank engine.

Belaugh Staithe

This quiet spot with public mooring lies at the end of a long and winding cul de sac off the road from Hoveton to Coltishall and is a wonderfully tranquil place to eat your packed lunch.

Platforms 2 and 3
You can see how each of the two tracks into Aylsham Station forks to allow
trains to draw up on either side of the two most frequently used platforms.

Technicolour

On a bright sunny day you can't miss No.3 2nd Air Division USAAF but it hasn't always been painted so vividly and used to be an uninspiring shade of maroon.

Buxton Station

This intermediate station is just a halt with a short platform and a bench on which to sit while waiting for the train and admiring the splendid views across the fields to Oxnead.

Opposite:
In the spotlight
No.9 Mark Timothy has very distinctive lines and appears frequently on the pages of this book.

Brampton Station

Jeff Riley indicates to the guard that he is ready to depart. Another halt with just a short platform, Brampton has the added interest of being able to watch trains pass one another on the loop just beyond the station.

Trackside photography

Readers should be aware that a number of images such as this were obtained by special arrangement and were captured from positions not accessible to the public. Additional safety measures were put in place for both the photographer and train driver.

And they're off!
With a burst of steam the 10.05 departs Aylsham with a coachload of passengers
for a tour of the Broads, their coach just visible in the background.

Primary colours
Blessed with yet another sunny day, the red and Caledonian Sky Blue paint job of
Wroxham Broad stands out vividly against the foliage of the trees at Wroxham Station.

Hoveton Hall Gardens

Both these walled gardens and a large area of the grounds surrounding Hoveton Hall and its lake are
open to the public and can be visited from Wroxham. More than 600 plant varieties grow here, attracting up
to 25 species of butterfly and the intriguing hummingbird hawk-moth as well as the hairy dragonfly.

The Spider Gate

This wonderful gate, in the form of a spider's web with the spider at its centre, is the entrance to the walled garden (opposite). Constructed in 1936, the gate is the work of Eric Stevenson from Wroxham whose wrought iron creations have been used in ten different cathedrals.

A friendly wave
There is something about the narrow gauge experience which instantly makes everyone more
friendly and communicative. A train will never pass you by without both adults and children giving you
a cheery look and a wave. When was the last time that happened to you on the M25?

Wroxham water tower

There are plenty of opportunities to capture images of the locos on their own, as well as with coaches, from the long platform at Wroxham.

Opposite:

Photos from the footpath

The footpath and cycle track run immediately alongside the track, separated by a wire fence, for the entire line enabling close encounters of the Bure Valley kind to be captured with the simplest of pocket cameras.

Synchronised snaps
There are numerous occasions during the timetable's busy Yellow Service period of late July and the whole of August when two trains can be snapped within 10 or twenty minutes of one another at a single location.

Cheerful staff
Full-time employee Martin Cogger, seen here in the capacity of guard, is clearly happy in his work.

Visual aids
Hardly difficult to see coming with its bright Golden Ochre paintwork,
No.3 makes use of its twin headlights for good measure.

Opposite:
Bridge over untroubled water
At this point along the line, just south of Buxton, it passes over the slow moving waters of the
River Bure, ruffled only by a gentle and very welcome breeze as temperatures soar. On the far
side of the bridge a set of steps provide access from the trackside footpath down to the path
along the riverbank, which makes a pleasant alternative to Coltishall.

Equal rights
As driver, Juliet also gets the job of manually pushing her loco round on the turntable.

Tribute

This is the sight which greets passengers during the middle part of the day as they enter the station at Aylsham. In between pulling the first train of the day and the last one, No.3 2nd Air Division USAAF is usually parked here by the station entrance. No.3 was named in tribute to 6,700 young Americans who died flying B24 Liberators from 14 airfields in the area during World War II.

No.8 Thunder
Seen here after topping up with water at Aylsham, this loco is known for having an unusually reflective paint job. It has just been overhauled and converted from being oil-fired to using coal.

Chalk and cheese
Well, coal and diesel anyway. While shunting at Aylsham, No.3 is seen
passing the coal bunker used for fuelling its sister locos.

Two way traffic
Movement along the line is controlled from the single signal box at Aylsham using radio communication rather than signals. In addition, clipboards with essential information are exchanged between the person manning the signal box and the guard.

Top up time

No.1 is filled up with water at Wroxham. It is one of the most widely travelled locos having operated
on the Fairbourne Railway, at Dudley Zoo, on the Romney Hythe & Dymchurch line, at Blenheim Palace,
on the Lightwater Valley Railway and at Steamtown in Carnforth.

Brampton

These attractive cottages are a stone's throw from the station. There is no car park at the halt at Brampton, unlike every other station (though Coltishall's car park is limited to about four vehicles). It is possible to park in the village but with a degree of sensitivity as the roads are only narrow.

Water Mill
This magnificent water mill can be found on the east side of Buxton on the road to Lamas.

Establishing shot

This is the term used for an attractive image which might lead a magazine feature and which contains all the relevant ingredients: in this case the station, water tower, and a loco complete with steam, all beautifully lit and complete with colourful foreground.

Viewpoint

Trying to find different viewpoints can sometimes be difficult. The station at Coltishall is several feet lower than the small car park and it is possible to look down on the line for a slightly different perspective.

High visibility

Any of the staff working at trackside, and indeed the author when taking these photographs, must wear a high visibility jacket or waistcoat. Interestingly, it has been found that orange works far better in the railway environment than the fluorescent yellow favoured by most emergency services and those involved with roadworks.

Opposite:

Lunchtime

Many of the passengers about to alight from this lunchtime arrival at Aylsham will make use of the restaurant here. Passenger numbers are radioed through from Wroxham when trains depart so that restaurant staff can assess how busy they may be when the train arrives.

On loan
The most economical and arguably the most distinctive loco used by BVR, No.9 Mark Timothy is actually on loan from its owner. Its livery makes use of a shade of paint called Madder Lake Red.

Opposite:
Into the light
A few minutes south of Aylsham a tunnel carries the line under the main road.
Blickling Hall is seen here emerging into daylight heading northbound.

Blickling Hall

The hall itself, as opposed to the loco carrying the same name, is seen here from the road and is situated just north of Aylsham. This magnificent 17th century Jacobean house with its gardens and park are open to the public and owned by the National Trust. The Long Gallery is said to contain one of the finest privately owned collections of rare books in the country.

Half the size, twice the fun
Based loosely on Indian Railway's 2ft 6ins gauge ZB Class, though only a half-sized replica, No.6
is 28ft long and 4ft 6ins wide and weighs in at 13 tons. It was purpose built for the line in 1994.

Round tower church, Brampton

Brampton's historic church has undergone many changes over the years. The original knapped flint church with its round tower dates back to the Normans but the tower top was added in the 15th century.

Caution
Warning signs instruct passengers not to stray off the platform at any station, and platform edges are clearly marked as a safety measure. Accidents can only occur when people ignore the advice given.

139

Time enough for a chat
Volunteer driver Paul Stubbins and full-time employee Martin Cogger acting as
guard both enjoy a chat prior to taking the 10.37 southwards from Coltishall.

Wroxham Broad

Not the loco with the same name but the actual Broad for once. Scenes such as this are typical of the area and just one of the benefits of buying a combined ticket for the line and boat trip.

Buxton Station
On one side of the station is a housing estate but on the other fields
extend into the distance, broken only by the occasional line of trees.

Aylsham turntable

The proximity of the platforms can be seen here, but you can actually get a closer view of the turntable in action from the car park which is out of shot on the right.

Finally . . .

On the final page I always try to use an image which sums up the subject of the book. In hindsight, it says something about my personal 'Bure Valley Experience' that I instinctively chose an image that, instead of depicting one of the steam locos as you might expect, actually conveys a great deal about the cheerful enthusiasm I encountered among the many volunteers and full-time employees.